EYE TO EYE WITH HORSES

Appaloosa Horses

Lynn M. Stone

Rourke

Publishing LLC

Vero Beach, Florida 32964

www.rourkepublishing.com

PHOTO CREDITS: All photos © Lynn M. Stone except pages 5, 13, and 21 © Kristen Reiter and page 18 © Daren Reiter

Editor: Robert Stengard-Olliges

Cover and page design by Tara Raymo

Library of Congress Cataloging-in-Publication Data

Stone, Lynn M.
 Appaloosa horses / Lynn M. Stone.
   p. cm. -- (Eye to eye with horses)
 ISBN 978-1-60044-580-4
 1. Appaloosa horse--Juvenile literature. I. Title.
 SF293.A7S857 2008
 636.1'3--dc22
                                    2007019092

Printed in the USA

CG/CG

Rourke Publishing

www.rourkepublishing.com – rourke@rourkepublishing.com
Post Office Box 3328, Vero Beach, FL 32964

2

Table of Contents

Appaloosa Horses

The Appaloosa is a popular American **breed** first developed by the Native American Nez Perce tribe. It's best known for its leopard like spots and other irregular markings in its coat.

Many Appaloosas have spots, like leopards and Dalmatian dogs.

A trail rider grazes an Appaloosa in the old Nez Perce country of the northwest.

The Nez Perce lived in the northwest, in what is now southeastern Washington, northeast Oregon, and western Idaho. They grazed their horses in the Snake, Clearwater, and Palouse River valleys. The word "Appaloosa" probably came from twisting the word "Palouse."

Appaloosas may have a solid coat (left) or the traditional spots and flecks.

For most of its history, the Appaloosa has been easily identified by its coat and other features. In more recent years, however, picking out an Appaloosa has become more difficult. Many Appaloosas now have solid color coats! Appaloosas have also changed in **conformation**—the way they are built.

This is the result of Appaloosas having been **crossed** to Quarter Horses, Arabian horses, and Thoroughbreds. Crossing one breed with another is nothing new in the world of domestic animals. The results may be useful, or they may create a problem.

APPALOOSA FACTS

Appaloosa's can have mottled or pink skin. The pink skin is speckled with darker colors.

Appaloosa's eyes have white areas, like people have; other horses have very little white.

The Appaloosa Horse Club accepts certain crossbred horses as Appaloosas. But not everyone wants big changes in the original Appaloosa type.

In 1991, the International Colored Appaloosa Association formed. It accepts only Appaloosas with two Appaloosa parents and traditional Appaloosa features. The goal is to bring back the traditional Appaloosa horse.

A roan blanket with spots colors this traditional Appaloosa.

The History of Appaloosa Horses

Spanish explorers brought horses to North America in the early 1500's. **Local** Native American tribes traded and raided for horses. Over time, horses spread northwesterly into Nez Perce country.

First brought to North America by the Spanish, horses eventually reached the northwest.

Like the Nez Perce, today's Appaloosa owners prize their horses' saddle qualities as well as color.

By the 1700's the Nez Perce were raising fine horses through careful **selective breeding**. They picked only the best horses as mothers and fathers of foals. Not all their horses were spotted. Color was not the Native Americans' only concern. They also wanted rugged horses that could be ridden for war, hunting, and work.

Meriwether Clark took note of the Nez Perce horses nearly one hundred years later on the Lewis and Clark Expedition. "Their horses appear to be of an excellent race," he wrote in his journal. "They are lofty, elegantly formed, active and durable...."

This Appaloosa stallion is a descendant of the "active and durable" Nez Perce horses of the 1800's.

In the 1860's, conflict arose between American settlers and the Nez Perce. The army tried to force the Nez Perce onto a reservation. Chief Joseph of the Nez Perce and his tribe fled with their horses. They traveled more than 1,000 miles (1,600 kilometers) in an attempt to reach Canada. They were stopped 40 miles (64 kilometers) short of their goal. A few horses escaped into the countryside. Some were sold. Most were shot by the army.

The annual Chief Joseph Trail Ride, an Appaloosa-only event, follows 100-mile (160-kilometer) sections of the Nez Perce retreat toward Canada.

Francis Haines helped restore interest in spotted Appaloosas.

By the 1930's the Nez Perce horses were nearly forgotten, but not by Francis Haines. He and his friends looked for Appaloosas and began the Appaloosa Horse Club.

Haines' search was successful. The club located several Appaloosas. Interest in the spotted horses grew. By the 1970's, the Appaloosa had become the third most popular breed in the United States.

Being an Appaloosa Horse

The traditional Appaloosa has a white ring around the iris of its eyes. It has spotted skin on its muzzle. It has hooves usually marked with black and white stripes. It often has a fairly short, thin tail, and it stands between 14.2 – 15.2 hands high (58 – 62 inches, 149 – 159 centimeters). Like other "cow ponies" of the West, the typical Appaloosa had a compact body, deep chest, and muscular thighs.

A traditional leopard Appaloosa shows its striped hooves and spotted muzzle.

Many solid coat Appaloosas show the influence of Arabian and Quarter Horse crosses.

Many of today's Appaloosas look much like Quarter Horses. The neck is lower. The head is shorter and more tapered. And, of course, many of the Appaloosas in show rings have no visible spots!

Owning an Appaloosa Horse

The Appaloosa became popular for two main reasons. It was **versatile** and it was colorful. It is still versatile. It can be a cow pony on cattle ranches. It can be a pleasure riding horse. It can also be used for long distance riding, short distance racing, and jumping.

Pleasure riders on the Chief Joseph Trail Ride stop to water their mounts.

Many Appaloosa owners aren't as concerned about the animal's color as owners once were. But even the Appaloosa Horse Club is taking steps to encourage the breeding of Appaloosas to Appaloosas. That—and the efforts of the Colored Appaloosa Association—should help the Appaloosas of tomorrow look more like the Appaloosas of yesterday.

More old style Appaloosa coats may be the wave of the future.

Glossary

breed (BREED) – a group of domestic animals within a group (such as an Appaloosa horse), having the same basic characteristics

conformation (kon FUR may shuhn) – an animal's body shape and size

crossed (KRAWSSD) – to have been matched or mated with another breed

local (LOH kuhl) – referring to anyone or anything of the immediate location

selective breeding (si LEK tiv bree DING) – the process of choosing an animal's parents

versatile (VUR suh tuhl) – able to do many things well

Index

Further Reading

Dell, Pamela. *Appaloosas*. Child's World, 2007.
Maass, Sarah. *Appaloosa Horse*. Capstone, 2005.

Website to Visit

www.appaloosa.com
www.kyhorsepark.com/imh/bw/appa.html
www.icaainc.com

About the Author

Lynn M. Stone is the author of more than 400 children's books. He is a talented natural history photographer as well. Lynn, a former teacher, travels worldwide to photograph wildlife in its natural habitat.